Ethereum:

A Guide to Ethereum Mining, Investing, and Trading for Starters

Financial Growth Publications

Table of Contents

Additionally, the information in the following pages is intended only for informational purposes and should thus be thought of as universal. As befitting its nature, it is presented without assurance regarding its prolonged validity or interim quality. Trademarks that are mentioned are done without written consent and can in no way be considered an endorsement from the trademark holder.

Introduction

Thank you for buying *Ethereum: A Guide to Ethereum Mining, Investing, and Trading for Starters.*

It is interesting to witness the emergence of a new era in history. The generations that live today have opportunities that only a decade ago would have been considered science fiction. Our generation now gets to usher in a whole new era that blends together technology with economics on a completely new level.

No doubt, you picked up this book because you have heard some things about the Blockchain, Bitcoin, and Ethereum. Perhaps you've heard about the amazing returns others have received from investing in these instruments, and now you want your piece of the pie. Maybe you've heard the story about the guy who paid for his pizza with Bitcoins, and now those two coins are worth more than $100 million today.

This book is not about any of that. The word about Bitcoin has already spread to the far reaches of the earth. This book is going to focus all of its attention on the number two cryptocurrency, Bitcoin's younger brother who has already made the scene in a very big way. However, it is not possible to talk about Ethereum without at least saying a little bit about Bitcoin, the coin that paved the way and opened the door for all other cryptocurrencies on the market.

But once you understand exactly what Bitcoin is, how the Blockchain technology is making decentralized applications so effective, then you will appreciate even more how Ethereum has taken the next evolutionary leap in cryptocurrency, you'll have an even clearer understanding of what to expect in its future.

There may be many reasons why you are interested in Ethereum. Perhaps you want to know more about mining it. In these pages, we'll discuss the pros and cons of mining, and how to get started. You'll learn the steps needed to get set-up. Where to look to buy the necessary equipment, and what you need to know.

If your interest lies in direct investment, then we'll talk about some basic investment strategies that have been very effective when claiming a stake in Ethereum and we'll discuss some things you should know about trading in this fast-growing cryptocurrency.

It is no doubt that the idea of cryptocurrency is new and unique and many are trying to find where they fit in this new global phenomenon. We hope that through the pages of this book, you'll learn enough information to at least find your place and take the initial steps that will help you to get your footing in this virtual world.

It can be very exciting to witness all the wonderful things that are happening in the world today, but it can be even more exciting to be a part of it. Very few people are satisfied with just being a spectator on the sidelines when they understand the impact of this type of innovation. If you're like most people, you want to be part of the game so you can reap the most benefits. If that's you, then let's get started.

Welcome to the game!

There are plenty of books on this subject on the market, thanks again for choosing this one! Every effort was made to ensure it is full of as much useful information as possible, please enjoy!

Chapter 1: The Birth of Ethereum

Before we can fully understand what Ethereum really is, we need to go back to the beginning and understand what money is and its original purpose. For centuries, money has been used as a means of transferring value from one person to another. It was a very effective means of keeping track of who owned what and was the next evolutionary step from the old barter system that many cultures once used.

The reason the barter system eventually fell into disuse was its impracticality. There were elements of the system that failed to take certain factors into effect. First, for an exchange to take place, the other party needed to specifically want the goods that others had to offer. For example, if you wanted to trade a plow for a cow, the other person had to want your cow. It also didn't take into account that each individual could set up his own value system, which wasn't likely to match with someone what another person believed was its true worth.

The introduction of money changed all of that. By having one central authority that determined a set value of the local currency, it served as a sort of equalizer so that value was a bit more consistent throughout a particular civilization. Once money became the common form of currency, it was monitored, issued, and managed by the governments.

This is the system we have all become very comfortable with and for thousands of years have used it with a great deal of success. Still, that doesn't mean that money itself didn't have any flaws of its own. Several problems resulted from the centralization of money. One of the main issues many faced was the need to use a central authority to transfer value from one person to the next. By using these central figures, users were often exposed to high fees, loss of privacy, and other governmental controls. In short, users often lost the ability to control and manage the funds that they worked for.

To understand this better, think about how you get paid for the work you do. In most cases, you go to work for the assigned pay period, but when it comes time to get paid, your employer does not just give you the money for the services provided. Instead, it is sent to a bank that is governed and regulated by the government; you receive a piece of paper that says exactly how much you earned. For you to access that money, you must first go to the bank and present some sort of government-issued identification or use a bank-issued card in an ATM machine before the money is issued to you. Before that happens, however, the government takes his cut, and the bank also charges its fees. All of that happens before you see your first dime.

If you want to pay the bill, then the same process happens. You must either ask the bank to send the specified amount to the merchant to cover your debt. Again, the merchant doesn't actually get the money directly unless the bank chooses to release the funds. At any rate, you get the picture. We may think we are in control of our money, but it is really in the hands of uninterested third parties who also want to charge phenomenal sums of money for the unwanted privilege of handling our money.

This kind of management, while proven to be more effective than the old barter system, has had its own share of problems. As more and more third party individuals start to get greedy, charging even higher fees, people became increasingly more desperate to find other options for managing their money.

Many saw the problem stemmed from the use of a centralized system to manage the money. Even when they used digital currency, as they often did with services like PayPal, Skrill, or Google Wallet, there was always a high level of risk. The exposure to hacking and other cybercrimes were very real, and there was still the lack of control for many who are forced to rely on the system. Their privacy and their security were often compromised.

The idea for a change came literally from the world-wide-web, which for the first time in our history, made it possible for everyone to access the same information whenever they wanted it. It laid the foundation for economic giants like Amazon, eBay, and Apple to build multi-billion dollar corporations.

Once people got a taste of more control, felt what it was like to manage their own funds, it was just a matter of time before it would evolve into a means of managing the economics of society. This was to be done through the introduction of Blockchain Technology. It allowed for the control of currency to be put back into the hands of those who actually own it, worked for it, and used it. It made it possible for people to exchange value without the constant overseeing eye of Big Brother watching. Blockchain Technology allowed people to reclaim and control what they were working for all along.

What Exactly is the Blockchain?

In the simplest of terms, a Blockchain is merely a digital ledger similar to the one used at your bank. It is a record of what values exist and who owns them. The difference between the ledgers that the banks and governments maintain is a matter of who controls it and who has access to it. A centralized ledger owned by the banks is available to only a select group of people whereas the Blockchain ledger is open to the public. More specifically, a Blockchain is actually open-source software, which means that anyone on the system can observe transactions as they happen. Nothing on the Blockchain is done in secret.

This raises a common question: if the information on the Blockchain is public, how is it that it can protect someone's privacy? How can it be public but the users remain anonymous at the same time? The answer is where cryptocurrency comes in. The method of digitally encrypting data related to each transaction makes all of this possible.

Once a transaction enters the system, it is encrypted so that privacy is not only maintained, but the details of the transaction are virtually unalterable. At the same time, every detail of the transaction is placed in a block, which is then delivered to every computer in the system so that no single entity is in control of its contents. By taking the role of the middleman in all currency transactions and placing it in the hands of an automated third party, it basically boosts security in a number of ways. How exactly does this work?

In our traditional system, the banks would control the ledger and would monitor when transactions occur and maintain that information on a single server. The Blockchain, however, takes the role of the bank and puts the verification process in the hands of a group of people who manage the automation of the system. The identity and any other personal data related to those involved in the process are encrypted leaving only the total amount of the transaction open to the public. Because of this encryption coding, it is the most secure way of transferring value ever used by the masses. So, while the information is public and easily accessible to anyone using the network, the details of the transaction, personal identity, and other private information is thoroughly encrypted in forms that are virtually impossible for cybercriminals to get at.

Why It Was Needed

The Blockchain has proven to be a major breakthrough for many. Even if you have a limited background in finance, it is easy to understand how this could be of significance to many people. When Bitcoin first introduced it, it took a while before the impact of its value gained attention.

Bitcoin was used to offer an alternative form of currency, one that would always exist purely in the digital world. It is a system that allowed users to transfer value from one person to the next bypassing the current system. While banks and other financial institutions, could issue you physical money in exchange for digital currency, Bitcoin could never be used anywhere except through the Internet.

Because of the Blockchain, users were able to easily send currency anywhere around the world without the aid of a third party. If you wanted to make a purchase, you could pay using Bitcoin in much the same way as you would pay for an online purchase for the same item. They could also perform transactions much faster because there was no need for validation from a centralized third party.

This process makes it possible for a form of peer-to-peer transactions to be made merely on the basis of trust between the two parties involved. While it is similar to a straight cash transaction, where two people agree on the transfer of ownership of an item, it differs in the sense that the details of that transaction are recorded in perpetuity on the Blockchain. The "trust" therefore, is based not just on a verbal agreement but also in the evidence of that transaction that is recorded in encrypted digital format.

Bitcoin, therefore, was a whole different animal. It was similar in form to other digital currencies, but by using the Blockchain format, it was no longer regulated by the governing bodies of whatever financial institution managed it. It also differed in the sense that no governmental institution would determine its value. Its ledger is totally maintained by the users of the network, and they are the ones that give it value.

It wasn't long before people began to perceive the true value of the Blockchain, which for a time was limited to the process of exchanging currency. People began to realize that the Blockchain could be utilized in others ways that extended far beyond that of finances.

It was from this type of innovative thinking that Ethereum was born. By taking Blockchain technology and using it in an entirely different way, users soon were able to create decentralized programs with far more complexity than Bitcoin.

What is Ethereum?

The creator of Ethereum, Vitalik Buterin, envisioned an open-source computer program that could be used as a platform for a wide range of programming capabilities. This opened the door for all sorts of innovative ideas to be put into practice without fear of your property being stolen. In essence, Ethereum's adaption of Blockchain technology created not just a platform of peer-to-peer exchange of currency but as a peer-to-peer transfer of computer programming. You can liken it to a collaboration of efforts in creating a single document; several people may have had some role in its final completion. The only difference is that Ethereum is still evolving. With each new addition to the code, new changes are being born.

The entire structure of Ethereum is exceedingly more complicated than Bitcoin's basic format of currency exchange. The transactions performed on Ethereum's network go much further than just an exchange of value.

It's Purpose

Two features make Ethereum stand out from other forms of cryptocurrency, the ability to create Smart Contracts and Distributed Applications (Dapps). These are the key elements of the Ethereum network. With numerous new applications already in use and even more still to be developed, these two features give us a clear picture of Ethereum's main purposes and serve as an impetus to its gaining popularity.

To put it in the most basic of terms, Ethereum is a decentralized platform used to run smart contracts and distributed applications without third party involvement. The network has zero risks of censorship, fraud, or any other type of interference that could prevent it from performing its tasks. With these smart contracts, a user can add just about anything to the Blockchain and know that it is secure and the terms of any agreement will be met without disruption.

Its coin, Ether is used to run the network and even to give value to work being done, but its applications can serve as a means to trade all manner of things that go far beyond currency. Through this platform, partnerships are being born every day. Most notably is a partnership between Microsoft and ConsenSys. Together, with the use of a smart contract, both their clients and developers can offer a single click, cloud-based Blockchain environment that can be utilized in all sorts of businesses.

It serves as a higher form of Blockchain technology that is similar in basic format to Bitcoin but does not share enough similarities to compete with its forerunner. With Ethereum, users can build and use their own decentralized applications meant to run with Blockchain technology in a way that is both adaptable to all sorts of business interests and flexible enough to be used by anyone.

In effect, while the two utilize the same Blockchain, they have two entirely different purposes. Bitcoin's main purpose is to provide an alternative means of exchanging value while Ethereum's main goal is to provide an alternative means of transacting all other forms of business.

How it Differs From Bitcoin

On the surface, the differences between the two are pretty clear. Ethereum is not and was never meant to be a form of purchasing power like Bitcoin, but the main differences lie it their technology. For example, the programming language is very different and unique to each coin. Other differences are found in the speed of transactions (Ethereum's transactions are completed in seconds compared to Bitcoin's minutes)

The most publicized difference is probably that Ethereum was never meant as a medium of payment but rather a means of creating peer-to-peer contracts and applications to facilitate the work developers need to do in creating DApps.

Chapter 2: How Does It Work?

Understanding the basics is easy enough but understanding how it works requires looking a little more deeply into the inner workings of Ethereum. One of the most common questions one might ask is how can you be sure that the automated system is working correctly to ensure that all transactions are performed as they should be. This is a very reasonable question. After all, banks go to great lengths to ensure that the people they use to verify the transactions you perform are not only well trained and qualified, but they also must be trustworthy.

The Ethereum Blockchain is made up of thousands of nodes (individual computer systems) located throughout the globe. When a transaction is submitted to the network, it is picked up and dropped into a pool where a miner will pick it up. The miner uses Ethereum's software to verify the validity of the transaction. To ensure that there is no chance of tampering or fraud, each miner is given access to the transactions at random.

Once the miner receives the transaction, he must apply a complex set of algorithms to verify their validity. This process may require a great deal of computing energy to complete. If the miner is successful in validating the transaction, it is added to a block (a compilation of all transactions made within a specific time frame); each completed block is added to the Blockchain. Each block has to connect to the block proceeding it, literally creating a chain. To form a block, there is a very specific pattern of rules that must be met.

Of course, that is the simplest explanation of how Ethereum works. However, the technology has quite a few moving parts that anyone considering investing in should come to understand and appreciate.

With every Ethereum application, the Blockchain keeps track of the most recent adjustment to any contract or document in the system. Each time a transaction is made, the data related to that account is updated and dispensed to all the nodes on the Blockchain.

The Ethereum Virtual Machine

Each time the program is used, the verified data is distributed to thousands of nodes in the network. Any contract written using Ethereum's smart contract programming language is then collected into a "byte code," which is read and executed by the Ethereum Virtual Machine (EVM).

Because the EVM is the part of the system that ensures security and the execution of all the contracts, it is extremely important to the success of Ethereum. Its focus is to 1) prevent Denial-of-service attacks and 2) ensure communication within the system can be completed without interference.

The technology behind the EVM is capable of automatically fulfilling specific tasks set out in the smart contracts. In short, the EVM is the automated system that self-executes stipulations encoded in the smart contracts. For example, if a smart contract is encoded with instructions to transfer title of a property to another person after a certain number of payments are met, it is the EVM that will automatically do that once the terms of the agreement have been complied with.

Smart Contracts

To fully grasp the concept behind smart contracts, we must go back to the Blockchain. One of the first things we need to realize is that we are not speaking of contracts in the same sense of the contracts that we conjure up in our regular business dealings. While the end result will be the same, we want to think of these smart contracts more as taking the place of our lawyers, accountants, and notaries.

The main idea behind them is that they must serve as a self-executing mechanism used to fulfill any agreements between two parties. They are specially written codes that perform specific tasks when they are told. So, a smart contract is actually a computer programming code that tells the EVM when to perform a certain task.

By implementing smart contracts to the Blockchain, it fosters a field of trust. This is one of the reasons why the miner's role is so important in the actual validation of every transaction that passes through Ethereum's network.

Swarm and Whisper

As you might imagine, storing all of this data would take up a lot of space. Being able to store code that consists of numbers and digits as with Bitcoin's simple platform is a far cry from the detailed data that must be kept in Ethereum's database.

Their solution to this problem comes in the form of Swarm, a decentralized storage branch in the network. Swarm's role is to function in the same way as Dropbox does, by providing a platform for users to store their data and share information. This will all be managed and controlled with a consensus algorithm that will verify not just the content but also to clear a path for those authorized to use it.

The advantage of this type of storage system is again its decentralization. Without any one single entity responsible for maintaining the data, there are no possible means for any individual or group to remove it from the system.

To that end, the future for this aspect of the Ethereum network is without end. Already, many are considering it as a place to archive records, historical documents, medical records, and other forms of data that could have immense value to succeeding generations.

Of course, this new storage system is in its early stages and is not expected to launch until the summer of 2018 along with a new consensus algorithm miners will use to verify data. As expected, the team behind Swarm's development is already at work reworking the entire network to incorporate not just its storage capabilities but also the synchronization and retrievability of all the data it is expected to store.

Since the new storage platform will be using the new proof-of-concept algorithm, it is expected to be completely compatible with other tools used in the Ethereum network.

With Swarm, users will be able to store medical records, property deeds, and any other type of document by using nodes to connect to the swarm network. Users will receive a swarm address that they can send to the other party in the agreement allowing them to access the documentation.

Whisper, on the other hand, another technology that is utilized by Ethereum is a communication protocol that allows Dapps to interact with each other. The Whisper protocol allows for peer-to-peer messaging to be passed along the network.

It is a system that will operate completely separate from the Blockchain but in conjunction with it. Whisper has a number of characteristics that will eventually allow it to become a standard feature for developers when they want to add a specific message to anything they are coding.

Whisper encrypts the messages in the same way that every other aspect of a transaction will be encrypted to ensure that not only are the contents preserved and protected but also the metadata as well.

This can serve as a huge plus for the users and for the developers. By not having free access to data, developers won't be held as liable for its protection. They cannot accidentally "leak" information nor can they be coerced into divulging it to any unauthorized individual.

One can think of it as an added layer of security for everyone concerned.

Sometimes referred to as the Holy Trinity, these three parts of the system (Ethereum, Swarm, and Whisper) when combined can produce a formidable network that will be hard for any centralized platform to compete with. No doubt, this added level of protection when used on the Blockchain can be an appealing option for many corporations that wish to at least divert some of their business affairs away from the traditional method of centralization that we have been relying on for centuries.

What Exactly is Solidity?

The Ethereum network brings all of this together using a unique programming language called Solidity. This high-level programming language is used to instruct the EVM on the protocols and demands of each contract that will have to be self-executed in the future.

Solidity is the scripting language, which enforces the verifying and enforcing the terms of whatever agreements are made and put into the system. All of Ethereum's source code is written in Solidity and remains consistent with the execution of every agreement.

Proof of Work

The proof-of-work (PoW) algorithm is the tool by which miners will be able to ensure that each block added to the chain is the only version of the transactions contained in it. It is also the tool by which unauthorized individuals will be prevented from hacking the system and sabotaging it in some way.

With the PoW, miners work to add the next block to the chain by solving a cryptographic puzzle. The first miner to solve the puzzle gets to add the block to the chain and in reward will be paid in Ether along with a small transaction fee.

Once they receive a transaction, they run the block's header metadata through a hash function to find the hash. The resulting hash must match the current target. Once the hash matches all the requirements, it must be checked and verified by another miner before it can be included in the Blockchain.

Using this encryption method, Ethereum creates a completely new block every 12-15 seconds, much faster than Bitcoin's new block creation time of once every 10 minutes.

It is very difficult to solve the solutions to the puzzles created by the encryption process, so it is practically impossible to cheat when working out the Proof-of-work algorithm. Each hash created must not only match with all of the transactions included in the block, but it must also match the block before it. Also, each character in the code has to have some sort of relationship with the other characters in the hash. This process creates millions of variables with only one possible outcome. It is the Blockchain's system for ensuring that no data has been altered or tampered with in any way. In fact, if even one figure is changed it not only affects the hash that was created but it will also affect every hash created after it.

Once the hash is created, it is added to the Blockchain, and the entire process begins again with the miner working to solve the next block in the chain.

While you may not understand every aspect of the Ethereum network, having knowledge like this can be very beneficial in understanding how the system works and why it is considered to be a platform for the ages. Deciding if you want to be a part of this world starts with understanding exactly what's involved in the Ethereum Blockchain and why so many people are intrigued by it.

Chapter 3: Who Should Invest in Ethereum and Why?

It is easy to see how Ethereum's prices have consistently increased since it was first introduced in 2016. Some reports are even showing returns as high as 3000%. Those kinds of reports are more than enough to stir up excitement about investment opportunities. However, like anything else, investing in Ethereum is not the best choice for everyone. There are several questions you must answer about Ethereum and about your own personal investment style before you can determine whether or not it is the right investment choice for you.

Let's first talk about Ethereum's potential in the cryptocurrency marketplace. One of the first things you want to determine is its path for the future. What things indicate that Ethereum will be around in the next year, five years, or even twenty years?

If you have been following the reports you probably already know about the Enterprise Ethereum Alliance (EEA), an organization set up specifically to connect Ethereum with many major industry leaders. Already large corporations like Microsoft, Santander, JP Morgan, Credit Suisse, and Brainbot Technologies are on board. They've partnered with the currency primarily because of its multi-purpose design that can be adapted to just about any industry.

These partnerships have also been an impetus for the rising value of the coin and are a major cause of the bullish trend we have been witnessing in recent months. According to many cryptocurrency experts, it is very reasonable to see the value of Ether continue to rise, especially as more and more larger corporations begin to utilize its capabilities.

Prediction for Ether's price predictions has also been very promising. According to many experts, if history is to repeat itself, the price of Ethereum is expected to increase to more than $20,000 per coin within the next year and even more beyond that. If you're looking for a long-term investment option then now might be the best time to get in; the prices are still low enough so you won't have to put up a significant amount of cash. You'd actually be investing at a low price before the bullish trends begin to rise. At the time of this writing, Ethereum's investment stats look extremely promising.

- Average Daily ROI   1.69%
- Average Monthly ROI   66.11%
- Total ROI   34,515.80%
- Volatility trailing 30 days   43.44%
- Volatility trailing 7 days   20.98%

If its track record continues like this, it is a strong possibility that Ethereum will be around for quite some time. For the moment, it appears to be an ideal investment opportunity for someone looking for a long-term situation. But the next question to answer is if it is the right opportunity for you.

Is Ethereum the Right Opportunity for You?

While there are always a lot of statistics and logic involved in making an investment decision, there is also the need to personalize the data and tailor it to your personal needs. Just as there are numerous investment opportunities, there are also more than a few investment styles and needs. The decision to invest in anything will also depend on the individual needs of the investor. To determine whether or not Ethereum or any other type of cryptocurrency is right for you will depend on where you fit in the whole scheme of things. To determine this, you need to understand your personal level of risk tolerance, your investment style, and create your own investment plan.

How to Analyze Your Risk tolerance

Risk tolerance is a term often heard but never fully understood, especially for a new investor. We often hear references to investment opportunities that vary based on a person's risk tolerance, but we first need to fully comprehend what it is before we can determine where we lie on the spectrum.

Several factors must be considered when determining your risk tolerance. One has to do with how much time you have to invest. It is a general course of wisdom that says that the younger you are, the more time you have to wait for your returns to come in. While many people think the returns they want to achieve when they invest they also have to consider the amount of time they have. If you are a young person, perhaps in your twenties then you would have a long-term investment horizon, but as you age, your investment horizon begins to shorten.

This knowledge will determine if you would want to invest in Ethereum or not. If you have a short investment horizon, you're probably going to be looking at opportunities that will require you to see results very quickly. Ask yourself...when will the returns be needed? If you need them quickly, you would want to take a more conservative approach to the investment. If your investment horizon is longer, you could probably afford to take a riskier stance with Ethereum, perhaps even trying some day trading or margin trading.

You also want to think about your risk capital. What is your net worth? Your net worth is simply how much money you have to spare. Simply list all of your assets and then subtract the total amount of your liabilities. This will tell you how much capital you are in a position to risk. Those with a high net worth will be able to take on more risk and can afford to take a more aggressive stance when it comes to investment choices, but those with a low-risk capital will need to be able to play it safe, so they don't lose too much and end up causing financial hardship.

Be careful not to fall into the trap that many investment opportunities present. It is easy to be drawn into riskier investment measures when you have a small amount of risk capital to work with. The idea of fast money or the opportunity to win big can be a powerful lure, but if you have only a little to invest, it is better to play it safe and build up your portfolio slowly. Once you've increased your risk capital, then you can venture into more dangerous waters for those bigger returns.

Next, you want to think about your ultimate goals. What do you want to get out of this decision? Are you setting up a plan for your retirement? Are you planning an around the world cruise? Or do you just want to build a nest egg that you can tap into later? Your goals will also factor in helping you determine how much of your money you are willing to risk. If you're saving for your child's college education, you'll probably be more protective of your money than someone who is planning an around the world cruise.

Finally, you want to think about your experience in investing, especially when it concerns cryptocurrencies. If you are new to this type of investment, you should proceed with caution. As you learn more about the market and how it moves you could take more chances with your money.

Investing in Ethereum is very much like investing in anything else. There are levels of investment risks that everyone should take. But once you know your risk tolerance the easier it will be to decide if investing in Ethereum is right for you and if it is, then how much of your money you are willing to risk to get those returns.

Knowing your risk tolerance is not just about the anxiety that naturally comes with a volatile market like cryptocurrency. It is about being able to balance your financial position and your goals and finding the right place for you to enter the market and with how much.

Determining Your Investment Style

Now that you know your level of risk tolerance, you need to determine what type of investor you want to be. You have probably already realized that understanding your risk tolerance has already allowed you to remove certain investment options you were already thinking about. Now, it's time to narrow that field down just a little bit more.

People tend to get very excited about investment tools like Ethereum. They see the meteoric rise in prices and they are drawn to them like a string pulling at their hearts. But when it comes to serious investing, that is exactly what shouldn't happen. To be successful in this type of move, it is important to approach it logically rather than with the fever pitch of adrenaline pumping through your veins.

Risk tolerance determines how much of your assets you are willing to risk to get a return on your investment, but your investment style reveals to what degree you want to delve into the market. There are at least three different major investment styles where most people fit. Of course, these can be broken down into smaller degrees so you might find yourself a blend of two but in determining where you fit it is important to understand these basic investment styles.

Passive: As an investor, you should first think about to what extent you trust the advice of the experts in telling you how to get the largest returns.

Those who want to lean entirely upon the counsel of professional advisors, and only follow the direction on when to get in or out of the market, or whether or not they should have a long or short-term investment would be considered to have a passive investment style.

These people have full confidence in the words of the experts believing that they have their finger on the pulse of the market and are in a better position to predict future movements.

Active: There are also those investors who want to do all the legwork themselves. They don't really trust the advice of others who may not know their personal situation. They make their decisions based on their own research and calculations.

Growth: Are you looking for a coin that is on the fast track and will grow exponentially over the coming months or are you willing to sit back and wait for a slower but more stable return on your investment? Those who are looking for a faster rate of growth will be interested in coins that are already showing faster growth rates and higher profit margins.

Value: The value investment style focuses on the price. They want to get in at a low price and sell at a higher price. The rate of growth is not necessarily that important. These people more than likely lean towards a long-term investment strategy because they are not focused on how fast the market moves; their only concern is that the market is moving in the right direction.

Capitalization: When it comes to stock investing, those companies with a small cap usually bring a better return on their investment because there is more room for growth. However, when it comes to cryptocurrencies, that is not the case. Small-cap coins are often more vulnerable to attacks because buyers can more easily manipulate the market. When it comes to investment style, any coin that is under one million in market cap is already in the danger zone, making them a much riskier investment.

The good news is that Ethereum is not a small cap coin, so while there are risks involved, they are in a much better position than many other coins.

It is very important that you determine your personal investment style before you decide to enter the market. It will help you to determine not just if you're going to invest in Ethereum but how much you plan to invest, and it may even help you to pinpoint a comfortable time to take the plunge.

Creating an Investment Plan

Now that you already know your risk tolerance and your investment style, it's time to create your plan. Whether you're a first-time investor or you've already dabbled with other coins, it is important to lay out on paper your expectations and milestones you expect to achieve.

You've probably already heard about the many rags to riches stories that are floating around the Internet, and many of them are true. However, those stories are not the norm for most people. While it is possible to achieve this type of success with Ethereum, it should not be without some sort of game plan.

By the very nature of the cryptocurrency market, it is never wise to invest all of your assets into one coin, even one as good as Ethereum. For that reason, you'll need to determine what percentage of your assets you want to put into Ethereum and what percentage you want to put in other coins.

Again, go back to your risk tolerance and try to determine what other coins will be able to support your acceptable level of risk and matches your investment style to decide which ones will be best designed to work in tandem with Ethereum. Many experts recommend that newcomers take a more conservative approach while experienced ones who know the market can afford to take a higher risk and dabble in something a little more dangerous.

Those with a low horizon will likely want to lean towards balancing their portfolio with more traditional and proven coins and those with a long horizon will more than likely lean towards some of the newer coins or ICOs.

Getting Ready for the Big Day

Before you can buy your first Ether, it is necessary for you to get prepared. Buying Ethereum is not the same as buying anything else. Certain things must be in place before you begin.

The Wallet

Because Ethereum is a digital currency, you will need to have a digital wallet to store it. Like any other wallet you might have, a digital wallet is primarily used as a depository for your cryptocurrency. However, it has other functions too that you will have to rely on from time to time.

Before you can begin to understand the role of the wallet, you have to grasp the concept of digital currency. Since cryptocurrency does not have any physical characteristics, your currency will exist in the wallet in the form of codes and numbers. What your wallet will actually hold are the private keys that give you access to those coins.

Every wallet comes with at least two keys (some have more) a public and a private key. The public keys allow the holder to send a portion of their currency to another user while the private key is to make sure that the transaction remains secure. Anyone who holds the private key has access to your coins.

This means that just as you wouldn't leave your physical wallet laying around for anyone to pick up, you must use the same diligence in protecting the keys to your digital wallet.

There is a wide variety of wallet options to choose from. The one you choose will depend on how you plan to use your Ether.

Software wallet

A software wallet is a program installed on your computer. You have total control of the wallet, and as long as you protect your private key, no one else can have access to your currency. Simply choose the one with the features you like and download it into your computer and you are ready to begin using it.

This type of wallet is about as secure as you can get but there are some vulnerabilities. They are only as safe as your computer. Because they are connected to the Internet they may be affected by malware and other cyber issues, so they are not always the safest in terms of protecting your currency.

Paper Wallet

Paper wallets are a means of protecting your private and public keys in a physical form. Once you have received your currency, simply print out the keys and store them someplace safe that is offline. As long as the data stored on the computer is deleted after you print out the details your money will remain safe.

The advantage of paper wallets is that all access to your currency is stored completely offline making it inaccessible to cybercriminals who may be looking for ways to access it. The drawback is that they are more exposed to environmental issues that could destroy the coin. By keeping the paper in a secure location where it can't be damaged by water, fire, or other environmental hazards you can be sure that your currency remains safe.

Web Wallets

Many exchanges offer web wallets to make it convenient to access your currency when you need it. Setting up a web wallet with the exchange you plan to trade with can be very convenient. Any earnings you make from the sale of coins are automatically deposited into your web wallet, and anytime you want to make a purchase, the money is drawn from your wallet balance just like when you use an ATM or debit card.

Obviously, convenience is the key advantage of a web wallet. With just a few keystrokes you can buy, sell, trade without any hassle. Using software or paper wallets means transferring the funds from your offline wallet to the exchange, which could take time. Considering the volatility of the cryptocurrency market, there are times when you have a very short window of opportunity to make a good deal.

Hardware Wallet

These wallets work on the same level as a USB port. They are small portable devices that can be inserted into your computer when you are ready to make a trade and removed when your transaction is completed.

Advantages of the hardware wallet are the convenience. Once your currency is stored, all you need to do is insert the wallet into a computer device hooked up to the Internet and perform whatever transaction you want to do. When completed, disengage your wallet and store it for the next time.

Exchange Wallets

Many new investors often wonder why they can't leave their coins on the exchange where they are trading. You automatically receive an exchange wallet when you open an account. However, there are some obvious risks associated with these wallets.

Not only do you not have control of your keys when you hold currency in an exchange account wallet, but they offer a third party service, and you are entrusting them with the responsibility of keeping your money safe. In addition, they are usually the primary targets for hackers and other types of cybercriminals looking to steal away with your coins. Without the structure of regulation behind them, they are extremely vulnerable on a number of levels. Ideally, you want to keep your coins on a platform that you have complete control over.

Generally, it is recommended to have at least two wallets, one hot and one cold. Hot wallets are those that you will use to buy, sell or trade with while cold wallets are those where you will store the bulk of your coins. These are kept offline where they are the safest, so there is a much lower risk of tampering or loss.

Once you've made the decision to invest in Ethereum, you should find the wallet you want to use. This needs to be done so that you have some place to deposit your funds when you make your first transaction.

For Ethereum, many people recommend the Mist Ethereum wallet. It is considered the official wallet for Ethereum. It is not the only option you have, but it has many characteristics that are ideal for the Ethereum investor.

- Access to your own private keys
- Easy to use
- A strong community backing it (if you have problems)
- It can be backed up and restored if your passwords or keys are lost.
- It is compatible with a number of different systems.

No matter which wallet you choose, you need to make sure that first, it is compatible with the computer you'll be using and 2) you have enough storage space to store it. The Mist wallet, Ethereum's official wallet, for example, takes up almost 10 megabytes of space. It will come in a zip file, and you'll need to unzip it and install it on your system.

Once the wallet is installed, your next step will be to launch it on your computer and sync it with the Ethereum network. It would be a good idea to find some detailed information about the wallet before you begin, as this will definitely simplify the process of getting set up. As a matter of fact, there are a number of YouTube videos that will walk you through the process painlessly.

Choose an Exchange

Now that your wallet is set up, you can start buying and selling Ether. However, you will need to know how to generate your wallet address so that the exchange knows where to deposit your Ether.

The good news is that because Ethereum is the number two coin on the cryptocurrency market, it will be easy to find an exchange that will allow you to trade them. Several factors must be considered when choosing the exchange. Just because most exchanges may allow you to trade Ether, doesn't mean they are all the same. Do careful research to find one that best suits your needs. Here are a few things you need to look for.

- Fees: one of the first things you need to find out are the fees the exchange will charge. It is nice to think that they'll just let you buy and sell for free but all exchanges work on a commission. Some will charge a fee for every possible use you have while others will not. You don't want to end up paying all of your profits to the exchange in fees.

- Location: Depending on the location of the exchange you may find that the way they do business will vary. Exchanges found in the western countries like the United States and Canada are often subjected to governmental regulations to protect your investment, but those found in eastern countries like China may have no regulations they are compelled to comply with. If anything were to happen, your money might be easily lost.

- Customer service: Some exchanges only have customer support via email while others may offer direct human-to-human chats. It is also good to find out if their customer support is in a number of languages. It could be difficult to work out a problem when no one can speak in a language you understand.

- Security: Find out exactly what security measures they have in place. The risk of losing your currency through cybercrime is high. Since most exchanges store their data in the cloud, if you choose to leave your money in your exchange wallet if something were to happen it could be impossible for you to recover if they don't have some sort of security measure in place. Exchanges are not insured with FDIC like banks and other types of financial institutions so once your currency is lost, or if the exchange folds, you may lose everything.

These are just some of the things you might want to investigate before you choose an exchange to work with. Chances are you'll think of more once you start interacting with them.

After you've decided on your exchange, you need to setup your account. Hopefully, the one you choose will be very user-friendly so you can navigate their system easily.

For newbies, an online wallet is the easiest way to get started. It provides you with an address for the exchange to send your currency to, but many are able to handle more than one currency. With online wallets, you can actually pay for other coins with crypto rather than exchanging your crypto for dollars and then use that money to buy a new coin. It not only will save additional steps but it can also save in fees too.

To open your exchange account, you will need to go through the signup process, which should be pretty straightforward. Depending on how much you want to invest, to begin with, they may ask for identification or other personal information. Once you've input all of the requested information, they will then ask you to go through a verification process; usually by sending a photograph of your identification, or uploading a picture.

Some exchanges will do this automatically, while others may have you wait for a day or two until they validate the information you've given them. So, if you're anxious about getting started with Ethereum, it is a good idea to set up your wallet and exchange well before you are ready to enter the market. There is nothing more frustrating than seeing the price right where you want it to be, but you can start trading because you're not set up yet.

It is important to remember that while the setup of a new account is pretty basic stuff, you should never forget your personal security measures when you're exchanging personal information online. It is true that exchanges get hacked from time to time, but the majority of cryptocurrency losses are usually the result of lack of care by the user. Protect your email account, your passwords, and any other security measures that are already in place. When you do this, you can greatly minimize the risk of your account being exposed or vulnerable.

Hopefully, you've picked an exchange that uses two-factor authentication, so it gives you an additional layer of security. Some points to remember as you go through the process.

- Use your real name and address

- Use your real phone number

- Choose a password that is unique. Don't settle for a password with five or six characters. Some exchanges require passwords that are at least 32 characters long that are made up of a combination of upper and lower case letters, along with numbers and symbols. The more complex the password, the safer your investment will be.

While every exchange is different, you can be expected to provide the same information, no matter which one you choose. The good news is that once all your information is verified and you've gone through the process, you are ready to start investing in your Ethereum.

Even though you plan to start with one wallet, in time you will likely find that you will need more than one (hot and cold) and you may find that you need to deal with more than one exchange. As long as you remember to get setup long before you need them, you should be fine.

Chapter 4: Analyzing the Market

Most newbies in the crypto world are getting into the market because they have heard many rumors about how much money there is to be made in this new technology. They've heard about the incredible profits of Bitcoin and those that follow along with it. Chances are if you're reading this book, you're doing so because of some rumor you've heard.

In most cases, they didn't have a definite plan. They just wanted to get in the market, buy some Ether, and wait for the price to rise. That is definitely one way to go, but there is an awful lot more than that to think about.

While there are quite a few websites that will do the analysis for you, it is extremely important that you at the very least learn to do some form of analysis yourself. There are two primary forms of analysis you can do before you decide to invest. A fundamental analysis involves getting a closer look at how the coin makes use of the Blockchain technology it is using. Basically, we want to make sure we get a good solid grasp of the foundation (or fundamentals) the coin is based on so you can determine its true value. Once you know the true value, then you can look at the price of the coin to decide if it is inflated or not. Technical analysis, on the other hand, is more focused on studying the actual price movements. A good percentage of the first two chapters of this book was an introduction to the fundamentals of Ethereum, but a fundamental analysis involves much more than just understanding how the system works.

Fundamental Analysis

Usually, fundamental analysis is used to decide which coin you want to invest in but even if you already have your sites on Ethereum, it still helps to do a fundamental analysis to determine if it is stable enough to support putting your trust in it. Ideally, you want to be able to do a fundamental analysis on any coin you want to invest in. Here are a few things you need to examine.

- Price stability: A coin's price is considered stable when the number of buyers and the number of sellers are the same. When you place an order to buy Ether, the price would naturally go up. If you place a sell order, then logically, the price would go down. If you have more buyers than sellers, the price will continue to rise and vice versa with sells. However, if the buyers and sellers are evenly matched, the price will be "stable." If the price is stable, it is actually the best time to put your money in the pot.

- How much security is needed to protect the Blockchain: The whole purpose of assigning hashes to a transaction is for security.

- Demand: Several factors can impact the demand for Ether. These include transaction activity, the amount of trading happening, and user adoption.

- Supply: this information is much easier to figure out than demand. The current supply of the coin is how many are in circulation at the time. You also want to look at the rate of new supply that is being released. Each time a miner adds a new block to the chain, he is paid in a certain amount of Ether, adding more to the supply.

- Major events: It is important to follow the news to see what major events are happening or are on the horizon. Because these events often affect the perception of the public, they can impact trade on a number of levels.

Once you have collected all this information, you will be able to create a picture of Ethereum, and a pattern should emerge. This type of data can be crucial in deciding at what point you want to put your money in the pot and when it might be best to hold back a little and wait for things to settle down a bit.

Technical Analysis

Conducting a technical analysis is much more detailed than a fundamental analysis, but it is just as important. In fact, many professional analysts believe that it is the technical analysis that can give you a better feel for the market at any given time. It is the tool that allows you to identify specific trends, and even predict future movements in the market. This skill is crucial for anyone who is interested in getting large returns on their investment dollars.

Technical analysis is about looking at the history of the coin. As you study the different charts and graphs, you will begin to see a consistent pattern of price movements you won't see by watching the price periodically. These movements can help you identify repeat patterns and what to expect in the coming days, weeks, months, and even years.

To perform a good technical analysis, you need to be able to make a few assumptions that serve as a valuable foundation on which to base your conclusions on.

- The current price on the market is a compilation of all information relating to the coin.

- Price movements are not random. They follow trends and patterns. Some patterns are long term while others may be short term but you are searching for those patterns.

- History is more valuable to your technical analysis than price movement.

- History often repeats itself, and therefore, price movements are predictable.

How to Identify Trends

The ability to determine the general direction a price is moving can be a valuable tool for any type of investment. Still, learning this skill can be quite difficult, especially in a volatile market like cryptocurrency.

However, by applying the assumptions listed above, you know that you can look beyond the present day movements and identify when a coin is about to make an upward move or start heading the other way. There will also be times when the price stays pretty much where it is with little to no upward or downward movement. These are called sideways trends. After studying the charts, you will notice that not only are there the up, down, and sideways trends but each trend has a time frame you must factor in. You might be looking at a short-term uptrend or a long-term sideways trend.

So, what are the tricks that will help you to identify these trends and what should you be looking for?

Moving averages: These are patterns that begin to average out the price of the coin so you can see exactly what it is selling for. By studying the moving average charts, you remove all the price fluctuations, which will make it much easier to see the true direction of a price movement.

There are several different types of moving average charts depending on the length of time you want to analyze. To get a moving average, simply calculate the average price over the specified time period you want to see. Depending on what your investment goal is you could do an average of as little as five days to as many as five years.

There is another moving average you might also want to study, the exponential moving average. It is a moving average that gives more weight to the most recent data. You will consult this average when you want to predict price changes as a result of more recent activity.

These are just a few of the strategies that you might want to think about when getting ready to buy Ethereum. When you understand the patterns that dictate the price movements, you will not only be able to enter the market with more confidence, but you'll also be able to better determine the right time and the right price to get started.

Where to Look for More Information

Knowing where to look to find the information to analyze is not always obvious. Go online, and you'll find hundreds of websites offering you all types of analysis, but you're never quite sure if they can be trusted or not. Cryptocurrency is an entirely new industry, and so are the many people who claim to be experts. It helps to know exactly where to go to find reliable information that you can base your assumptions, predictions, and decisions on.

The White Paper: One of the first places you want to go is the white paper. This is a detailed proposal created by the development team, which details the actual purpose of the coin as well as the mechanics. You won't need this information when doing a technical analysis, but it is very useful for your fundamental approach.

Slack Channel or Blog: Sometimes the white paper can be very technical and is full of complicated jargon that you may not understand. When you have questions, you can go to the slack channel or the coin's blog. This is where the development team interacts with the community and is the perfect platform for clarification when you need it.

Reddit – Steemit: These are public forums where you can feel out how the community actually feels about the coin. You might be surprised at the things you will learn when you're on these sites. It is one of the best ways to determine if there is enough support for the coin or if there is a growing sense of doubt about its future. As you read through these sites, you may hear questions raised that you may never have thought about or you may get better clarification on something that you were still trying to grasp.

It can be a challenge to learn how to analyze any cryptocurrency. There is a lot of information to sift through, and if you're not a detail-oriented person, it may begin to feel overwhelming. However, as you grow in your knowledge of these details, it will eventually become second nature to you, and you'll be much more comfortable in making your predictions.

Chapter 5: Ways to Make Money with Ethereum

Now that you have laid the groundwork for your Ethereum investment, you are ready to get started. For most people, the idea of investment is to buy low and sell high. This is a basic and fundamental rule that will carry you a long way. However, this is not the only way you can make money with Ethereum. In fact, you'll be surprised to know just how many different ways money can find its way to you through Ethereum. However, for this chapter, we're going to give you the three primary methods that have worked well for investors so far. Mining, Investing, and Trading.

Mining

Probably, one of the most important factors in the Ethereum Blockchain is the mining process. While you do need to know your way around a computer to be a miner, statistics show that earning money as a miner is actually more profitable than direct investing when you do it right.

The challenge, however, is that to mine you may need to invest in some pretty special equipment that may set you back a pretty penny. While you can mine with a CPU or a personal computer processing unit, the speed at which it moves could cut the amount of money you can make.

GPUs, on the other hand, tend to work as much as 200 times faster than your personal CPU and the faster it works, the better your chances of making money.

You will also need to download specific software to get started. So whatever system you plan to use, you want to make sure that it will be compatible with Ethereum's network. The good news is that you no longer need to download the full Ethereum Blockchain (now more than 20GB) to get started, nor do you need to deal with those cumbersome line miners with manual instructions anymore.

That said, you will need to invest something in getting your mining system setup. If you're not willing to shell out for quality hardware, your odds of generating a good income will be seriously curtailed. Still, the potential for profits is very good now. Below is a list of some pretty good reasons why people have chosen to mine Ethereum.

- It can serve as a great way to subsidize your current income
- It's an easy way to obtain Bitcoins. You can trade Ethereum for Bitcoin.
- Ethereum is a great entry coin opening the door to the cryptocurrency market.
- You can have your own voice on the Ethereum network through the mining process.

These are not the only reasons why you might want to consider mining but just a few to start you thinking. Because of the payout for every block solved, the idea of mining for Ether can be very tempting. However, it is a very technical approach to entering the cryptocurrency market and is not for everyone. If you are interested in learning more about the mining process and how it works, we'll go into more detail in the following chapter.

Investing

By and large, the majority of people who want to enter Ethereum's world will be investors, and this is for a good reason. Of all the money making ventures concerning cryptocurrency, investment is probably the most direct approach.

Those who choose to be investors realize that it is a game of numbers, but it is also psychological game as well. Learning how to predict what the public will do in any given situation can be an interesting endeavor, especially when it concerns money.

Successful investors are those who are diligent when it comes to studying charts, keeping up with the news reports, following social media, and keeping abreast of all sorts of things that might have an impact on the price of a coin. They are not the people who check the exchanges every day to see how the price has changed but they are those who are content to look beneath the surface to find out why the price has changed and to determine what might happen in the future.

Statistics show that Ethereum's price has increased 5,700% in the past year. The novice investor looks at those figures and says wow! I want to be a part of that and jumps into the fray without checking further. The savvy and cautious investor wants to know what caused the price increase and whether or not Ethereum will be able to maintain it and grow from there.

If you're trying to decide if investing is the best option for you, there are four different investment personalities; see if you fit into any one of these categories. Understanding your personal investment personality can help you to decide which investment strategy is going to work best for you when you're ready to put your money down.

1. The Preserver
2. The Accumulator
3. The Follower
4. The Independent

The Preserver: This type of investor is not a huge risk taker. His concern is in maintaining what he already has. The preserver closely monitors his assets and is very conscientious about protecting their losses. He is slow to make decisions mainly because he wants to avoid the possibility of making mistakes that could cause him to lose money in the end.

If you feel that you are a preserver, then you will be more interested in long-term investment strategies. When looking at Ethereum over an extended period of time, you will notice that while the price fluctuates a great deal in the short-term, the general trend is upward giving you a better chance of profit in the long-term.

Short-term investments for the preserver are risky because of the volatility of the market. Prices may see extreme lows and highs all in the same day. Preservers tend to be very emotional when faced with any type of loss and may be inclined to pull out of an investment too soon and lose out in the end.

The Accumulator: The accumulator is more interested in amassing wealth. They are more likely to be in control of their investment decisions and are willing to take risks. These are the people who study the graphs and charts diligently and are very confident in whatever conclusion they come to. Most accumulators have already seen success in other ventures of their lives and can easily transfer their experience in analyzing situations and coming to the right conclusion to their investment practices.

One problem the accumulator often faces is his overconfidence. Because they have had a history of success, they approach investing in cryptocurrency with the idea that they will always make the right choice. The result is that with the cryptocurrency market, there is extreme volatility, so the odds of miscalculating are even higher than with any other type of investment tool.

The Follower: This is the person who doesn't have a lot of confidence in his ability to gauge the market, so he tends to follow the advice of others. He is also easily swayed by exciting news or interesting stories about what a currency is doing. The follower rarely has any ideas of his own and generally depends on others to tell him which strategy he should take.

His greatest challenge has to do with the following the crowd mentality. He will readily pool his money with others simply on the basis of the idea that someone else says its good. This can present a major problem because often, by the time he hears about a profitable investment opportunity, it is already too late to take advantage of it. He may get in on an upswing in prices just before it begins to fall again. This strategy often leads to losses that could affect your overall plan.

The Independent: The independent investor is just like it sounds. This is the person who has his own ideas and strategies and is not afraid to steer away from the pack. These people are much more interested in the process of investing and can study the market in minute detail. They are very analytical and critical, and they have the confidence to stand on their own in any decision they make.

Their greatest challenge is their confidence. They tend to rely too much on their own thinking process and are not as willing to listen to and accept the advice of others, which can cause them many problems and often a loss of money in the end.

With each investor personality, there are always advantages and disadvantages. As long as you understand what type of investor you are and what your negative drawbacks are, you can create a plan of action that will help you to overcome the obstacles that are naturally a part of your particular investment personality.

Trading

Most people are guilty of using the words "investing" and "trading" interchangeably. And while there are many similarities in the thought process, they are very different tools.

If you've done any trading on the stock exchange, you will likely be very familiar with the art of trading Ethereum. You will need to become very adept at analyzing charts, and predicting future price movements. The trader must always do extensive research so that he can make well-informed decisions, and avoid giving in to the temptation to react to the volatility of the market.

However, that is where the two begin to diverge. When trading on the cryptocurrency exchange, your goal is to concentrate your efforts on buy and sell orders. When you place an order to trade, you are predicting that the price will go up or down and your payout comes when the market price reaches your prediction.

Successful traders have very specific characteristics in their personality. First, they are able to look at a chart and a graph and see beyond what s written on the page, they are able to see the big picture, connecting the past with the future to identify potential trading opportunities.

Second, they are very logical thinkers and are skillful analysts. They look at every detail with a critical eye and are capable of seeing possibilities where many others cannot.

They are extremely organized, are able to make decisions quickly, and are capable of following through despite what others may think or say. It takes time to become a good trader. You have to commit to a daily ritual of trading and studying charts and graphs consistently to develop that critical eye that will see all the possibilities that may not always be hidden in full view. The most successful traders are those that have developed their strategic skills and are good at planning. They are not only able to predict market movements with a high rate of accuracy, but they are emotionally balanced enough to make quick decisions under all sorts of market conditions. Whether the market is moving up or down, they know exactly how to make the most of the movement so they can achieve financial success.

Whether you decide to become a miner, investor, or trader, the possibilities of making money with Ethereum are very good as long as you recognize the risks and do your research. Those who choose to rush into the market and try to take shortcuts will definitely suffer the consequences.

Of course, these are not the only ways one can make money with Ethereum, but these are the most common and the most successful. So, now that you understand your personal investment style, you know exactly how you want to make money with Ethereum, let's take a look at these options in a little more depth.

Chapter 6: Mining Ethereum

While Bitcoin and Ethereum both exist because of Blockchain technology, there are a lot of differences that need to be understood. If most of your education about mining revolved around Bitcoin, then you're going to find something entirely different here.

One of the first things you'll discover is that Ethereum runs on Ether, so when you choose to invest, you're actually buying Ether, not Ethereum. For the miner, Ether is the reason he works on the Ethereum network.

While Ether is a form of currency, it is used in a very different way than Bitcoin. With Bitcoin, you can spend or trade it in a variety of ways, but Ether can only be used on the Ethereum platform. When clients use a smart contract on Ethereum, they pay for this service with Ether. From the miner's point of view, it is the means of greasing the wheels of the network. It is also the form of payment a miner will receive. So, when you are mining on the Ethereum platform, your ultimate goal is to acquire Ether by validating transactions on the network.

Why Do It?

There are a number of reasons why you might want to mine Ether rather than just buy it outright. For each person, that choice is different. It is based on your personality, investment style, specific circumstances, and your financial position.

No one can tell you that you should or should not mine Ether. It is a decision you must make for yourself. However, there are several common reasons why people might want to consider taking on this type of endeavor.

First and foremost is the money. For every successful block, you add to the Blockchain you are paid in Ether. If you're looking for a way to get into the market, this might be it.

How much you make will depend on your success rate at solving the blocks. You will have to decide beforehand if you feel that you can make more from mining Ether than you can from making an outright investment. It is important that you factor in the cost of the equipment you will have to obtain as well as the cost of power. Please note, while it may cost a lot to get set up with your mining rig, it is a one-time cost. After you've started, it is just a matter of how successful you will be in mining those coins.

Another reason you might want to consider mining Ether is to give support to the network. The more miners in the system, the more reliable it will be. This will naturally cause the price to go up, and you'll make a profit.

People also mine as a way to accumulate more coins over the long term. As the price of the coin continues to rise, so will the value of the Ether you've earned. It could end up being a pretty significant bottom line for you and a huge boost to your personal net worth.

I'm sure that you can come up with plenty of other reasons for mining Ether that haven't been discussed here. The main idea though, is that it will serve as a means to boost your personal net worth, to increase your income, and give you personal satisfaction that you are supporting a whole new economic system.

How to Get Set Up

Unlike other cryptocurrencies that require a very specific collection of hardware to mine, Ethereum's mining can be done on a wide variety of platforms. Even someone with a home computer can have a successful attempt at mining Ether. That's if their home setup meets certain specifications.

The biggest obstacle that Ethereum miners face is how to balance the cost of powering their equipment with the value of the Ether they receive. When you're new to the mining process, the best way to make money is by joining a mining pool. However, you still have the option of setting up your own mining rig yourself and working independently. In this chapter, we'll discuss both options so you can have a pretty good idea of how well each one works.

Hardware Needed: Since Ethereum does not use the same consensus algorithm as Bitcoin, the hardware must also be different. If you've been mining for Bitcoin in the past, you should know that the ASIC hardware you have will not work with the Ethereum network.

This is good news because it opens the door for more people to mine that do not have the money to lay out for that kind of expensive equipment. To set up your own mining rig, here are the things you will need:

- A motherboard: This is what will make it possible for all the different components to communicate with each other.

- A Graphics Card: This is the part of the system that processes the consensus algorithm.

- Adequate Storage capacity: You will need to have enough storage space to download the Blockchain and all the transactions that have been previously verified.

- Memory: You will need to have at least 8 GB of memory and possibly more. The files on your system will be consistently growing so whenever possible, opt for the higher memory.

- Power Supply Unit: This will generate the power you need to run your rig.

- Ethernet: Your mining rig will need to be connected to the Ethernet to process transactions correctly.

Of all the components needed to set up your rig, the Graphics Card is the most crucial. If you want to increase your chances of making money, you can invest in more than one Graphics Card. The more you have, the better your chances of being able to solve a block. It is important to recognize though, that the more equipment you have, the more power you will need to expend. So make sure that it balances out. It might be best to start with one card and add later after you have found some level of success in the endeavor.

For the most part, mining Ether is primarily done on the equipment you have. When you have a computer that can run 10,000 different possible permutations, it is easy to see that it is difficult for a solo miner to compete even under the best of conditions. However, there are a few things that can make your equipment run more efficiently, which could increase your chances of finding the right solution to the blocks that need to be mined.

1. Download Geth. This is the application that will allow you communicate with the Ethereum platform.

2. Unzip the file and transfer it all to your computer's HDD. In most cases, this will be the C: drive.

3. Execute the installation

4. On the command terminal, type in 'cd/' into the command prompt.

5. Create a new account on Geth.

6. Create a password, write it down and store it someplace safe.

7. Let Geth link up with the network. This is the action that will begin the download of Ethereum's Blockchain and sync your computer with the global network.

8. Download the mining software. Ethminer is a favored one on the Ethereum network, but there are others.

9. Install the software

10. Repeat step 4

11. In the new terminal window, type 'cd prog' and tab.

12. Go to the Ethereum mining software folder and type in 'cd cpp' then tab and enter.

13. To begin mining, type in 'ethminer-G' and press enter. This step will start the mining process.

These are simple basic setup procedures. However, there could be some variations depending on the type of equipment you have. Once you are all setup, test out the system to make sure that you are getting the most out of your equipment.

How to Do It

Getting the equipment setup and synced with the Ethereum network may take some time and it will require you to have at least a basic knowledge of how this type of hardware works. However, if you have some background in this area, it shouldn't be a difficult process. Just make sure that you follow the guidelines for the type of equipment you purchased so that you reduce the odds of complications from using incompatible components.

Once you're set up, and everything is communicating well with the network, you are ready to get started.

The idea of using the term "mining" came into play because of the comparison to the 19th-century gold mining. While a miner's primary goal is to validate transactions on the Ethereum network, the work they do also produces new Ether that can be used in the system or later traded for other cryptocurrencies or exchanged for traditional fiat currency.

This happens when the miner is able to figure out the unique hash of a block. A block is a collection of data that details the information pertaining to all the transactions completed within a specific period of time. Every new block created will have a unique alphanumeric string that has to meet certain characteristics.

- It must connect with the previous block

- All characters within it must be interrelated.

- It must contain a combination of alphanumeric characters along with symbols.

The detailed math behind this process creates a hash that works like a digital fingerprint for each block, no other block will have the same hash.

The idea of making money from mining can be exciting, but mining is not as simple as it sounds. It is not as if you're given a set of blocks and told to decipher these hashes. Instead, it works more like a competition. The details of the transactions are dropped into something called a pool, and the miner must take them from there. The challenge is that there could be hundreds of miners who are working on the same block. The one who is rewarded is the one that solves it first. This means that it is often the case that you are working on a particular block and another miner solves it. At that point, you must go back to the pool and begin the process all over again with another block. As a result, there could be days or even weeks before you are able to solve a single hash and collect your Ether.

Miner's serve very specific roles on the network. Aside from confirming transactions, they are the key players that protect the network from those who would like to cheat the system. They make sure that every transaction that is approved is authentic. They are also on the front lines protecting the network from numerous forms of cyber attacks, and they keep the massive decentralized machine functioning.

Types of Mining

There are several different types of mining setups you might want to think about. The first is what is called a home farm, which consists of all the mining equipment located in a single location. This type of mining is very expensive, as it requires the miner to setup and pay for an entire mining rig themselves. The good news is that the equipment necessary for mining Ether can be used for other purposes so if later on you decide that you want to give up on the practice, it has some resale value.

Another type of mining is referred to as cloud mining. This type is for people who do not want to spend a lot of money to set up an entire mining rig in their own home. Instead, they can mine remotely and simply share the processing power.

Caution is warranted when working with cloud mining; because you are not in control of the entire process, you are also not in control of the expenses you will incur when choosing to mine. The equipment you use is not your personal property so you may find you have to pay out more than you bargained for.

If you choose to use cloud mining, there are a few things you need to be aware of.

- Be wary of any group that promises you huge profits
- Make sure that you will have access to technical support when you need it
- Check them out thoroughly before you join. You can read reviews and monitor any chatter you may hear in the mining forums
- Always make sure that you follow whatever security protocols they have set in place.
- Never let anyone know where the mining farms are located.

Mining equipment can be costly. For this reason, not very many people choose to make money mining. It is not only expensive to acquire the needed hardware, but it is also expensive to run it. This makes it a vulnerable target for thieves and others so if you choose this route, it is necessary that you maintain a certain level of anonymity to protect your investment.

Is It Worth It?

Mining is not for everyone. Those who do well in this endeavor are those who can comfortably haggle with suppliers, and has enough computer knowledge to put the equipment together themselves. To make the most out of your equipment, you want it to last a long time. Here are a few suggestions that could extend the life of your equipment.

- Adjust your core voltage usage by setting it below zero. Try dropping it all the way down to -100. That will reduce the amount of energy your system will use when mining.

- You can also lower your core clock to bring down the temperature. This will also save on the wear and tear of your equipment.

- By applying overclocking at system startup, you won't have to go back and set it again after your system starts running.

Because a miner relies heavily on the efficiency of their equipment you need to do all that you can to extend its life. Probably the greatest enemy to mining equipment is heat, so anything you can do to lower the temperature and reduce power usage will not only help your equipment to work better, but it can also make it last longer.

The ability to make a success of mining is dependent on two things: the cost of the hardware and power. Returns are not consistent, and they are dependent on the price of Ether at any given time. Because of the extreme fluctuations in the market, a certain amount of Ether one month could be worth a great deal but the next month could be significantly lower, or higher. Still, if you have the right setup and a good energy source, it is possible to make a pretty good income from it.

There are several ways you can enter the mining system and the decision as to whether the cost of getting set up is worth it depends entirely on you. Weigh the costs of your initial investment in equipment, the amount of time you will have to dedicate to it, and the other costs and then make your decision.

Chapter 7: Investing in Ethereum

Investing in Ethereum is probably the most favored way of getting into the market. Often, people look at Bitcoin and are fully excited about its growth and how well the world has adopted it over the past decade. Then they look at Ethereum and end up scratching their heads a little bit.

They understand that it is taking a step away from Bitcoin's monetary system and using the Blockchain in another way, but it can be difficult to fully understand the power of this new type of currency. Still, with Ethereum gradually inserting its way into the world's consciousness, there are some pretty clear reasons why it is getting so much attention from investors all over the globe.

Why Do It?

There are a number of good reasons why you might want to consider buying your way into the Ethereum network. As more and more people begin to understand the extent of its capabilities it is gradually gaining in popularity. Over the last few years, we have witnessed Ethereum move from near obscurity to the number two coin on cryptocurrency exchanges.

Its value continues to rise. From its small beginnings only a few years ago, a single Ether now sells for more than $1,000.00.

It represents the future of business. Predicted to change the whole way we create agreements between parties, it has opened the door for more industries to find new ways to utilize the Blockchain.

Unlike other altcoins, purchasing Ether is very easy. It is found on nearly every exchange around the world. Other coins do not have the same recognition so can often be hard to find. Ether, however, is usually exchanged on the same platforms as Bitcoin making it easy to buy and sell, the ideal situation for any investor.

While Ether can only be used on its network, over the next few years more and more people are seeing its value. As the demand for it increases, so will its price, which can make a very good profit.

Making the First Buy

The good news is that investing in Ethereum is relatively easy. Unlike mining where you need to acquire a great deal of equipment, buying Ether is almost as easy as making a purchase on Amazon. You've already set up your wallet, and you've found your exchange. As far as preparation goes, that's all you need to do.

However, to make money as an investor, you need to buy and sell your currency. There are several ways to do this, but before we get into the details of this, we'll talk about making that very first buy; the one that gets your foot in the door so you can start to make money.

When it comes to making that first buy, it can be very frustrating with all the requirements some exchanges ask for, but once you do, you'll be glad you did.

How you make that first buy will depend on how you plan to pay for it. If you're planning on using fiat currency, you will have to set up an account with an exchange that accepts it. Some of the most popular exchanges that have good reputations are Coinbase, Coinmama, Polenix, and Kraken. As you do your research you will find quite a few other exchanges to pick from; just make sure that you thoroughly check them out before you give them all your personal information.

Once you've set up an account and connected a payment plan with it, it's as easy as hitting the buy button on your dashboard and following their instructions.

However, if you plan to pay for your Ether with Bitcoin or some other type of cryptocurrency, you need to find an exchange that will accept coin pairs. Most of the major exchanges will accept the BTC/ETH pair but make sure before you don't waste your time trying to make a buy when it is not possible.

Simple Investment Strategies

One of the easiest ways to get into buying Ether is just to buy it. This strategy is called by several names: Going Long, Buy and Hold, and even one investor refers to it as the way of the Samurai. Whatever you choose to call it, the idea is very simple. Buy the Ether and just hold onto it until you see the value increase.

This is the perfect investment strategy for beginners since it doesn't require constant vigilance and a major commitment of time pouring over charts and graphs. This doesn't mean that you have to do these things, but you won't have to be as focused on these tasks as you would with other forms of trading.

Because this strategy has a pretty high-profit potential, it has already attracted countless investors. However, that doesn't mean that it comes without risk. Even more stable and established coins will experience losses from time to time so you will still have to monitor the market regularly, looking for signs that the price will fall and take your profits with you.

However, if you learn to follow the trends and understand the patterns, it is possible to circumvent many of those pitfalls and get a pretty sizable return on investment.

When you choose to go long, it should be for at least one year. By holding the funds for that long, you avoid the chaotic up and down price fluctuation that often happens in a volatile market, and you aim for profits resulting from the natural upward mobility that the cryptocurrency market experiences in general.

Experts recommend that every investor should invest between 30-50% of their cryptocurrency portfolio in more stable coins like Bitcoin and Ethereum, and this is one of simplest ways to do this. But what other strategies could you use if you want to take a more aggressive approach or you want to pull in your profits a lot faster?

Buy and Diversify

While signs indicate that Ethereum is definitely a keeper and its future looks very promising, it is important to keep in mind that it is only one of over a thousand cryptocurrencies on the market. Ethereum's history is enough evidence to show that one day another small and obscure coin could also break out of the ranks and bring Ethereum some heavy competition.

That is proof enough that you don't want to leave all your eggs in one basket, no matter how good the conditions may seem. A way to hedge against that is to exchange some of your Ethereum for other assets like Ripple (XRP), Ethereum Classic (ETC), Dash, or Litecoin. This is a good strategy that can provide some buffer on the off chance that Ethereum may falter at some point in the future.

Going Short

The very opposite of going long is going short. When you go short, you buy your Ether in the same way, but this time your focus will be on taking advantage of the volatility of the market.

Investors that prefer to go short are looking for a faster return on their investment, which means that they will get in and out of the market in much less time. Rather than waiting for an entire year to cash in their returns, they may wait for a few days, weeks, or months. They watch the prices carefully in search of the right time to get out and claim their profits.

With this investment strategy, timing is crucial. The price you're aiming for may only be on the exchange for a matter of minutes, sometimes only seconds when the market is especially volatile. Instead of periodic monitoring of the charts and graphs, extensive research, and constant vigilance are necessary to make this strategy work.

While you need to have a goal for every time you invest, it is important that you know when you hit your mark. If your predictions are wrong, you also need to know at which point you will bail when it comes to taking a loss. Of course, no one expects to lose when they are investing so when the price drops, the tendency to ride it out may be very strong. *"If I can just hold on until the price recovers"* is the thought running through many people's minds. However, if you have an escape plan for this situation, you are less likely to be overcome by this kind of reasoning, and you already know where you will get out of the market even before you get in.

Rebalance

Rebalancing is the act of reviewing your investment portfolio after you've had a chance to earn a few profits. Remember, the make up of your portfolio was created before you started investing. If you had a smaller cash flow or were in debt, your approach to investing was probably pretty conservative. However, after you've earned a few profits, it would be wise to review your financial position to determine if you can readjust your investments. Perhaps, you can pull some of your profits from other coins and put more of them into Ether, or you may want to siphon off some of your Ether profits and store them in another investment tool.

Rebalancing should be done periodically as you achieve each of your goals to make sure that you are maximizing your profit potential. As your profits increase from your investment decisions, you will gain more if you practice rebalancing from time to time. This review of your financial situation should be done at least once a year, perhaps twice a year if you are bringing in higher profits.

Dollar Cost Averaging

It's also a good idea to look at how much you invest. In many cases, people make large purchases of coins at a single time, but if you don't have that kind of money laying around, you can also try dollar cost averaging.

Dollar cost averaging consists of dividing up your investment dollars and making regular payments over an extended period of time. Depending on the amount you wish to invest, simply take the total amount and divide it up over a specified time period. By making regular payments this way, you actually average out the total cost of the Ether you buy.

There are many benefits to this investment strategy. First, you are not as easily affected by the constant fluctuations of the market. By averaging your investment over time, you gain the benefits of buying more Ether at a lower price than you would if you had made a one-time investment. Also, you won't be affected as much by the constant price fluctuations that constantly occur in the market.

You also reduce your risk of getting into the market at the wrong time. Because your investment is based on an automatic system, it won't matter how much the price swings from one period to the next. It will keep you from jumping ship too soon when unexpected things arise. On the other hand, if you stick to this strategy religiously, you might also miss out on getting in at the right time as well.

This is the perfect tool for the less experienced investor. It takes the emotion out of the venture, but it does come with some drawbacks. As you become more familiar with navigating the market, you'll probably want to gradually step away from this method and try your hand at some more hands-on practices.

Diversify

While Ethereum is considered a good investment, it is always recommended that you never put all your eggs in one basket. No doubt, buying Ether should be a good part of your investment portfolio, but you should also try investing in other coins at the same time.

Most people view Ethereum and Bitcoin as the more stable cryptocurrencies, but Ethereum's platform itself opens the door to other coins that can be introduced through its network. Consider investing in some of the other tokens that are being offered on Ethereum's network. You might find yourself on the ground floor of another new cryptocurrency that will change the way the world sees things.

Setting Limits

The whole idea behind studying the charts and graphs, following the news reports, and engaging in chats is so that you can have enough information to predict which way the market is going to move. While this is a very good strategy, it is important to remember that no matter how much you analyze, study, and research there will be times when your predictions will miss their mark.

Even experts will make mistakes. It is easy to get caught up in the countless stories of all the people who have made a prediction about what the price will do and have hit their marks exactly. What you never hear about are the hundreds of others who also made predictions that were totally off the mark. It happens often when investing in cryptocurrencies.

While you can't make accurate predictions 100% of the time, you can prepare ahead of time for when you fail (which will happen); this can be done by setting limits. Often referred to as stop/loss limits, you can put them in place each time you purchase your coins.

The idea behind it is simple; if you predict that the price of Ether is going to rise in the coming weeks, you will buy your Ether at the expected entry price and then watch to see if your assumptions come true. However, if your predictions fail and the price drops, you set a stop/loss limit at a certain price. This will automatically trigger a sale of your Ether if the price falls too low.

This strategy prevents you from losing all of your investment in a single time. It allows you a chance to recover if you make a mistake. By selling your Ether if it falls to a certain point, you can always reenter the market if the price reverses later on, but you have protected your assets in the meantime.

By taking this step before you make your first purchase, your crypto portfolio is strengthened enough to weather those really rocky times when the market may unexpectedly go off the charts.

Keep Your Head

Even though Ethereum is a strong profit maker today, it is important that you take a practical approach to investing. It is easy to get excited about its success up to this point but this is a highly volatile market, and the potential for things to change is always present. With that in mind, it is important to keep emotions out of the investment strategy.

Never invest, even with the best of intentions, without a specific plan in mind. You must know the exact conditions when you want to buy and when you need to sell. With those thoughts already ingrained in your head, you have a better chance of surviving the rollercoaster cryptocurrency ride. Here are a few suggestions of things you might want to keep in mind to help you prepare for your first venture into cryptocurrency.

- Buy low and sell high. Avoid waiting for the price to keep going up so you can get more. The bottom could fall out, and you could lose everything. When the price has reached your target, sell and take your profits. You can always reenter later and take more profits then.

- Be patient.

- Always look at the big picture. When you look only at price, you can easily be duped with a false picture of what's really happening.

- Be consistent. Don't change strategies every time the market changes you'll end up losing out in the end.

- Try not to invest too much of your portfolio in a single currency.

- Never own only Ether, diversity is the best way to hedge against a market drop.

- You should have a good reason to buy and an equally important reason to sell.

- Make it a habit of checking prices at least once a day, and if you're only going to check once a day, make it the same time every day.

- Listen to advisors but have your own opinion.

- Make use of your stops to protect yourself from losses.

- Always know the risks.

- Avoid inflated promises of tripling your wealth in a day. While these things have happened in the past, rely on the more practical and realistic possibilities the market can offer.

- Remember, there are no guarantees that you will be successful.

Investing in Ether is a relatively easy thing to do. Sometimes, it is so easy that people will forget the risks involved. By keeping your head and taking a methodical approach to your investing, you have a much better chance of success in this type of market.

Chapter 8: Trading Ethereum

If you are more of the adventurous type, you might consider trading your Ether. This is not the most favored way to make money as it exposes the investor to a lot more risk than simply buying and holding. Because of its high level of risk, trading is not the best tool for everyone.

Trading is a bit more complicated than outright buying and selling. The trader actually is placing a bet on whether or not the price will increase or decrease. For example, one might conclude that the price of Ether will get stronger against the US dollar, or you may choose to bet against another cryptocurrency.

If you expect that Ether will see an increase in value, then you will place a bet with the expectation that the price will go up. However, if you think it will decrease in value, then you will bet accordingly.

There are many advantages to trading. Because you are not actually buying the Ether, you do not have to put up the entire amount of the investment you're considering. You can open yourself up to wider profits without risking losing all of your investment.

On the other hand, traders who choose to stay in the market for longer periods of time are more subject to losses than an investor would be.

To be successful in trading, you must be very familiar with market movements, its history, and its patterns. It takes a certain mindset to be successful in this type of money-making venture.

Who Does It?

Trading is difficult and often hard to understand. People who do not have a good technical background will find themselves struggling to master the concept of trading. It is also a highly stressful way to make money, and so those who are prone to getting excited will have a hard time following the basic tenets of a successful trader.

There are certain characteristics you might find in successful traders. Consider these to see if your personality fits in with these psychological aspects of a successful trader.

Lack the Normal Excitement About Cryptocurrency: Most people, when they hear about all the money to be made in the digital world are easily excitable and quick to throw their money in the pot. The trader, however, will hear those stories, build his interest, but want to do more research before making a decision.

Willing to Follow an Authority: If you lack adequate knowledge about cryptocurrency, you will be more inclined to listen to experts who had already had some success in trading. Traders are impulsive, but not impulsive enough to follow every story, but if they find someone who has a proven track record to show them the ropes, they will usually follow suit.

Does Not Have to Do Something: The cryptocurrency market is constantly moving. The volatility of the market can make it very unpredictable. Sometimes, the only way a trader can make a profit is to do nothing. For most newbies, they feel they have to do something to be successful, however. They must be buying or selling to keep their interest. Traders can gauge when it is a good time to do nothing, and just wait to see what the market will do.

Trading can easily become an emotional endeavor. Its fast paced movements, sudden market changes, and the rollercoaster highs and lows are enough to drive even the most sane person crazy. The person who chooses to become a trader will have to stand completely still in an environment of chaos, analyze the constant flow of input and find the small kernels of valuable truths to use as a basis for when they get in and out of the market. They have to be able to resist the FOMO (fear of missing out) and make decisions without being easily influenced by all the rumors and stories they will hear.

It is not something for the faint of heart, but if you can withstand this kind of pressure, it can be a highly profitable way of getting a huge return on your investment while putting up only a small stake in the total cost.

What It Means

Trading any type of cryptocurrency is very similar to what one does when involved in a Forex Trade. Unlike investing, where you buy at a certain price and wait for it to increase, trading is buying against another currency.

In Forex trading (foreign exchange) you are literally exchanging one currency for another with the expectation that your chosen currency will be of higher value in the future. This means that when you trade Ether, you are looking at other currencies to see which one will be stronger in the coming days or weeks.

Right now, the top two digital currencies today are Bitcoin and Ethereum, so there isn't very much competition between the two. So, the Ether trader will be looking mostly at fiat currencies to make his profits. The challenge for Ether traders is that Ethereum is not like any other cryptocurrency on the market. It isn't designed to take the place of another currency. You won't see anyone using it like they would fiat currencies so the valuation of it in comparison to dollars and cents can be very difficult and unpredictable.

This is where much of the risk is in predicting the movements of Ether against other fiat currencies. There is an unknown variable that the trader's mind must compensate for. Everything with Ether is not down in black and white, and therefore it makes each decision much more vulnerable to risk than many other more clearly defined altcoins.

Trading Strategies

There are quite a few trading strategies that can work well with Ethereum, but first, you need to understand the basic steps for executing a trade on an exchange.

Once a trader has decided where he thinks his best chance is for making a profit, he needs to place an order on the exchange. When he wants to "buy" into the market, he places what is called an open position. When he wants to "sell" he places a close position. Pending orders are those he places to happen when certain conditions are met. Regardless, each type of order is to be used in the process of buying and selling Ether.

It is strongly recommended that traders take advantage of using stop/loss or limit orders to protect themselves from a higher exposure to risk. Rather than buying or selling on the exchange, you place a market order instead. Once placed, it will be carried out at the price that occurs immediately after it is placed. If you, for example, place an order to buy, you must also set your limit at the same time.

It is a little different if you place a sell order. While the market buy order is set at the asking price, the market sell order will be filled at the bid price.

When placing these orders, you won't be as concerned with price, but you will need to stipulate how much you are buying. The main concern, at this point, is something called "slippage," which is the difference between the price you expect to pay and the price that you may end up paying. While in most cases, this may not be a large amount, because of the constant fluctuations in price it very well could turn out to be substantial. This usually occurs when there is a lot of activity happening on the exchange at the same time. As long as you understand this is a possibility, and you have prepared for it, your trade should be successful.

Margin Trading

Margin trading is based on a fairly simple concept. You are making the same trades as you would with the basic trading platform, but you are not staking the entire order yourself. You pay a percentage of the total cost of the order (the margin), and the rest is provided by another entity, usually the exchange or a brokerage house.

So, if you have $3,000 to invest, that would be your margin. The total amount of your order will depend on the percentage of your margin. For example, if you have a 1:3 margin, your $3000 would make up a third of the total investment. This is a great way to get more exposure to profits, but it also exposes you to greater losses as well.

This type of investing carries the highest risk. Because the market is constantly in motion, anything is possible at any time. The trader has a chance to earn much greater profits in a shorter period of time, but his exposure to risk is off the charts. Keep in mind that the higher the leverage, the lower the risk, so a leverage of 1:2 will be much better than 1:5. There are some exchanges that will offer leverages of 1:20, but it might be best to be very wary of such opportunities. The chances for massive profits are very real, but the exposure to losses are so great that you may find it is not worth it.

Also, keep in mind that you will be expected to pay interest on the borrowed amount. This interest is usually compounded on a daily basis so it can mount up very quickly. This is one reason why traders are so active in the market. They get in and get out very quickly. The longer they stay in, the more interest they have to pay which could easily eat up their profits before they even get a chance to see them.

If you fit the margin trading personality and you'd like to give it a try here are a few suggestions that could help you increase your chances of success.

- Buy in after you see the price has had a significant drop.

- Close your position only when you have a profit of 50% or more.

- Or close your position when you've seen a loss of no more than 20%.

As we said before, trading, especially margin trading, is not for the faint of heart. Your key to success is in micro profits and not the big haul. Traders are happy with an accumulation of small earnings that build up over time rather than that one big trade that will be the win all for everything they've done.

Day Trading

Day Trading is another high-intensity profit-making venture. It is the art of getting into the market and getting out on the same day. The number one rule of day traders is to never leave your money on the market while you sleep.

It takes great skill to become an effective day trader. It requires a major investment of time to constantly monitor the market to determine your entry and exit points. Most will sit in front of their computer screens for hours at a time as they monitor their situation and make strategic decisions. This type of trading is for those who are prepared to be very active in the market from the very beginning. If your goal is to earn a more passive income, then day trading is definitely not for you.

Some people, however, have found a compromise to the day trading strategy. Because it is in and out on the same day, they choose to trade on a regular basis but not necessarily every day. They may choose one day a week to participate in active trading and the rest of their time can be dedicated to other things.

Trading is one of the most complex forms of investing you will find, especially in the cryptocurrency market. Those who are the most successful at this have built up the skill over years. Many that go into trading cryptocurrencies were traders in other markets and carried their skills over to this new investment tool. If you decide you want to try trading Ether, make sure that you do thorough research from reliable sources before you begin.

Chapter 9: What to Expect Going Forward

The world of cryptocurrency, once thought to be a passing fad, is here to stay. With only a decade of history behind it, we have become eyewitnesses to an economic revolution that is just now taking wings. Coins like Ethereum have proven that when a coin has a good idea and strong community support that it has the power to change the status quo.

Whether you decide to embrace this currency or not, it is undeniable that it has great potential for our future. In just a few short years, it has grown to the number two spot on exchanges all over the world.

There are many good reasons why people seem to be drawn to it. While it is a powerful moneymaker, its unique technology that has gone beyond what we might imagine. The idea of taking the Blockchain and utilizing it in entirely different ways could be compared to the concept we all went through when we first learned about the Internet. Who would have imagined when the Internet first appeared that we would have social media, email, instant messaging, Skype, or any other of the myriad of things that it has been able to do.

Ethereum's future is similar. While it didn't invent or introduce the Blockchain to the world, we have no idea what Ethereum's smart contracts and Dapps will accomplish in the future. It's Ether can and will be used for countless other things in the coming years, some of them will defy our imagination.

Just as you see with other peer-to-peer networks, it's all about the architecture, the infrastructure, and the technology. Ethereum has accomplished all of that to open up a whole new battery of opportunities. Who knows where this technology will go in the future, but unlike other cryptocurrencies we see today, there is room to grow in unimaginable directions, and as a member of the Ethereum community, you will be able to join along for the ride.

Conclusion

We have finally come to the end of the *Ethereum: A Guide to Ethereum Mining, Investing, and Trading for Starters*. When it comes to Ethereum, there is a lot that could be said, and we have only touched on the basics of the information available.

The future of Ethereum is very promising, not just because of its ability to catapult business methods in a thousand different directions, but because it is allowing us to grow and move from an archaic economic system that has been heavily slanted to favor a small percentage of people and give power back to those who rely on it.

Just as we've seen revolutionary changes in our history, the changes that Ethereum and Bitcoin offer will reveal secrets that we couldn't possibly be able to predict. We have only just begun to grasp the power of Ethereum, and what it will do and those who join its community now will have front row seats to the show.

Think about it, in only a few short years, Ethereum has changed the way people think about business and as a result has become the highest traded currency on the market. If ever there was a time to make a decision and attach your future to something new and exciting it is now.

Finally, if you found this book useful in any way, a review on Amazon is always appreciated!

www.ingramcontent.com/pod-product-compliance
Lightning Source LLC
Chambersburg PA
CBHW071229220526
45468CB00002B/784